Blowout

PITT POETRY SERIES
ED OCHESTER, EDITOR

BLOWOUT

Denise Duhamel

UNIVERSITY OF PITTSBURGH PRESS

Published by the University of Pittsburgh Press, Pittsburgh, Pa., 15260

Copyright © 2013, Denise Duhamel

All rights reserved

Manufactured in the United States of America

Printed on acid-free paper

10 9 8 7 6 5 4 3 2 1

ISBN 13: 978-0-8229-6236-6

ISBN 10: 0-8229-6236-5

CONTENTS

ONE

How It Will End   3

Duper's Delight   5

If You Really Want to   6

Madonna and Me   8

Mack   12

Tina and the Bruised Hearts   14

Takeout, 2008   16

Ritual   21

Recession Commandments   22

Heartburn   25

An Unmarried Woman   27

TWO

Kindergarten Boyfriend   31

Fourth Grade Boyfriend   32

My Shortcut   33

Lower East Side Boyfriend   35

The Widow   37

Loaded   39

Cleopatra Invented the First Vibrator   41

My New Chum   42

A Different Story   44

You're Looking at the Love Interest   46

Or Wherever Your Final Destination May Be   48

Courtship   51

Worst Case Scenario   52

And So   54

Old Love Poems   58

Expired   60

THREE

Little Icaruses   63

Violenza Sessuale   64

My Strip Club   65

Victor   66

You Don't Get to Tell Me What to Do Ever Again   69

Self-Portrait in Hydrogen Peroxide   71

Proposal   73

Ten Days before We Meet, I Dream You   75

I Read   78

Long Distance Relationship   79

Sleep Seeds   81

Having a Diet Coke with You   83

Ode to Your Eyebrows   89

Acknowledgments   91

Blowout

One

How It Will End

We're walking on the boardwalk
but stop when we see a lifeguard and his girlfriend
fighting. We can't hear what they're saying,
but it is as good as a movie. We sit on a bench to find out
how it will end. I can tell by her body language
he's done something really bad. She stands at the bottom
of the ramp that leads to his hut. He tries to walk halfway down
to meet her, but she keeps signaling *don't come closer.*
My husband says, "Boy, he's sure in for it,"
and I say, "He deserves whatever's coming to him."
My husband thinks the lifeguard's cheated, but I think
she's sick of him only working part time
or maybe he forgot to put the rent in the mail.
The lifeguard tries to reach out
and she holds her hand like Diana Ross
when she performed "Stop in the Name of Love."
The red flag that slaps against his station means strong currents.
"She has to just get it out of her system,"
my husband laughs, but I'm not laughing.
I start to coach the girl to leave her no-good lifeguard,
but my husband predicts she'll never leave.
I'm angry at him for seeing glee in their situation
and say, "That's your problem—you think every fight
is funny. You never take her seriously," and he says,
"You never even give the guy a chance and you're always nagging,
so how can he tell the real issues from the nitpicking?"
and I say, "She doesn't nitpick!" and he says, "Oh really?
Maybe he should start recording her tirades," and I say,
"Maybe he should help out more," and he says,
"Maybe she should be more supportive," and I say,
"Do you mean supportive or do you mean support him?"
and my husband says that he's doing the best he can,

that's he's a lifeguard for Christ's sake, and I say
that her job is much harder, that she's a waitress
who works nights carrying heavy trays and is hit on all the time
by creepy tourists and he just sits there most days napping
and listening to "Power 96" and then ooh
he gets to be the big hero blowing his whistle
and running into the water to save beach bunnies who flatter him,
and my husband says it's not as though she's Miss Innocence
and what about the way she flirts, giving free refills
when her boss isn't looking or cutting extra large pieces of pie
to get bigger tips, oh no she wouldn't do that because she's a saint
and he's the devil, and I say, "I don't know why you can't just admit
he's a jerk," and my husband says, "I don't know why you can't admit
she's a killjoy," and then out of the blue the couple is making up.
The red flag flutters, then hangs limp.
She has her arms around his neck and is crying into his shoulder.
He whisks her up into his hut. We look around, but no one is watching us.

Duper's Delight

According to a body language expert on *The Big Idea,* a relationship is over
when one of the parties shoots a look of contempt at the other.
I turn to the TV—I was folding clothes—but it's too late.
I miss the visual cue the expert calls "a micro-expression." I'm curious
if it's a facial tic, a certain way the eyes flick or squint.
But she's already onto the next topic: *always turn
your bellybutton toward the interviewer if you want to get a job.*
Doesn't that mean you're turning your genitals toward the interviewer, too?
The host Donny Deutsch is nodding, his long arms open,
his palms toward the camera, which means he's receptive.
And I wonder about my husband's contempt, my own flinches,
what we say to each other with our faces. I call him
to come and hang up his shirts. When I point to the TV,
he tells me our twitches are nothing
but impatience, recounting examples of the stress
we've both been under of late. My husband smiles, a duper's delight,
the kind of grin the expert says indicates a liar
who takes a secret pleasure in his fabrication.
He looks away, another sign of a deception. His bellybutton
is at a 45-degree angle from mine. I'm dizzy again,
a condition for which I've diagnosed myself
on emedicinehealth.com. My husband is sick
of my whining, says it's only the heat from the dryer, but I know
it could also be my sinuses, anxiety, maybe symptoms of a stroke.
This morning an arrow of light fluttered in the corner
of my right eye. The image shone like an exit sign. All my blinking
and rubbing couldn't send it away. I can't tell you
exactly when the glowing projectile disappeared,
but I can tell you when my husband did,
exactly six days later, on September 10th.

If You Really Want to

The little old ladies at the condo whisper every time I walk past—
her husband left, did you see his face on TV, he's in some kind of trouble, I wonder
what their problem was, he always seemed like such a nice guy, maybe
he left her for someone else, maybe he's gay, maybe she cheated on him
and he found out, the police were at her door asking questions, the mailman
heard he was some kind of white-collar criminal, I heard he beat her,
the doorman told me she was crying . . .
                                                    The whispers get so bad that I'm afraid
to go to the local hair salon to tend to my wiry roots, my stress-straw hair,
so I can go back to work. I ask for the earliest appointment, climb into the chair,
looking past myself in the mirror to the ladies who file in behind me. I'm ready
to be asked, ready to tell my story, the one-sentence version I've practiced—
I'm going through a painful separation. The sentence is designed to gain pity,
to stop the questioner in her tracks.
                                                    As Mildred foils my hair for highlights,
I notice the group of old women decidedly ignoring me, huddled around
the coffee pot, crying. Their friend has jumped from the 26th floor. *She was depressed,*
one says, *and I told her, honey, get your medicines checked.* So sad, so sad for her husband
who knew something was wrong when he woke up and felt the breeze
from the balcony. She'd opened the sliding glass door and pulled out a step stool
so she could climb over the railing.
                                                    Imagine, just that step stool and her glasses
on the balcony tile. When her husband looked down, the maintenance men
were covering her body with a tarp. *If you really want to kill yourself,*
the most stooped lady says, *no one can stop you.* It had been a long month of threats,
my husband's suicide posts on Facebook. Someone (a former student) actually wrote
on his wall, *If you really want to kill yourself, take all your pills with milk*
so you don't throw up and then tie a plastic bag over your head.
                                                    The dye
stings my scalp. I guess my student thought my husband was joking around.
Maybe he was joking, a sadistic joke to make us all worry. *Don't do it!*

We all took turns writing to him. *Get to a hospital!* The lady who jumped was 80
and jumped naked. Mildred shakes her head and says that suicides tend to take off
their glasses before they kill themselves. Maybe that's because
it is like they are going to fall asleep for the last time
                                                    and they're used to leaving
their glasses on the nightstand. Maybe it's because they don't really want to see
what they're doing to themselves. Maybe they're afraid their glasses will shatter.
The old ladies feel guilty. The husband feels guilty. The children and grandchildren
are on their way. I feel guilty myself. When I wouldn't take him back,
my husband asked me to send him a warm coat. When I wouldn't take him back,
he asked me to send him his glasses and Bausch & Lomb contacts.

Madonna and Me

Madonna and I went through
our divorces
around the same time
and I followed her and Guy Ritchie
on perezhilton.com
as a kind of therapy

I mean if Madonna was getting divorced
it couldn't be so bad right
and she'd be OK and I'd be OK

Guy Ritchie was walking away
saying he didn't want her money
because he was a macho British dude
unlike my husband
who was neither macho nor British
and wanted every cent he could get

I kept wanting my guy
to take a cue from Madonna's Guy
I wanted the two to meet in a sweetshop
in London where they could bitch
about how Madonna and I
were so manipulative and controlling

Guy complained Madonna wouldn't allow
pastry in the house and I tried that rule too
since my husband had diabetes
Guy was underrated as was my ex
who thought himself more talented
than I as surely Guy thought
himself more talented than Madonna

or her Guy and my guy
could meet at a pub and pick up
younger women who would say
I don't know how you put up with that
and the new women would puff up the egos
that had been flattened
by Madonna and me with our big voices
hogging the spotlight

the press turned on Madonna
and wrote that she slept in a plastic suit
her body lubed up with wrinkle cream
that she and Guy never had sex anymore
but I think that suit may have been a lie

I didn't have such a suit
just old tee shirts and ratty shorts
I wore as pajamas
that my husband hated
because the shorts had paint stains
and the elastic waistband
was pretty shot and I'd dress up
for poetry readings but not for him
and what kind of wife did that

a wife tired of working two jobs
while her husband worked none
and maybe I was a workaholic
like Madonna who keeps touring
even though she'll never be able
to spend all her money

I had to work to support us
work just to survive
but the truth is
I was also happiest working
away from my husband
whose body left an imprint on the couch
like a chalk outline at a crime scene

and why didn't I dial 911
when it got really bad
Madonna didn't either all those years ago
when Sean tied her to a chair
though maybe that never happened
and it was just a Hollywood rumor

and even Madonna
who talked about everything
never talked about that
because that kind of stuff just doesn't happen
to strong women like Madonna and me

or it happens but we write
"deal with the situation"
on the bottom of our to-do list
and then throw the list away

it's easier to just step on a stage
or have the students
pull their chairs into a circle
for the poetry workshop
in that small room
where they will love you

or at least need you
to speak about their poems
and they will say *thank you for helping me*

and you will feel that even though
you can't help your husband anymore
you can help a few people
and they can help you
as you step into the applause

Mack

I'd never seen a truck so up close, felt its heat, the word MACK in caps at my left shoulder. I was trying to cross Houston Street to get to Second Avenue. It was three or four in the afternoon, right after the mail came, and I was going to a café to write, my laptop strapped across my back. I'd had an argument with my husband because I'd just opened our bills and he'd ordered porn through our cable company when I was away. He'd rented five or six movies—it was over $50. We didn't have $50 extra, we barely had the money for basic cable. He said, *I only watched a few minutes of each one, honest; then I went back to the Discovery Channel.* I screamed—what a boob, what a waste of money. But more importantly, I thought, why does he need to watch porn? What was wrong with him? What was wrong with me? Looking back at my journal entry about this day early in our marriage, I see now that I miswrote porn as prom. Even now, after all these years, I feel like I'm never going to truly get it, that I'm destined to become some bumbling *Golden Girl* Rose Nyland who doesn't understand anything, especially men. When I complain to my friend, she tells me even her girlfriend likes porn. It used to freak her out but now she just says, "Eh, so what?"

And now, my husband and I won't grow old together as I once thought we would, in our favorite booth of our favorite Miami Denny's, eating the senior specials, eggs and bacon. Now he has his porn and I have my word games. He's remarried, a McHusband, a Machiavellian who likes watching porn on his Mac like other Macks. He chews on macaroons, macadamia nuts, a new wife's macrobiotic macaroni salad. I sit outside under a mackerel sky crocheting immaculate macramé.

But that fall afternoon in New York, I guess I just wanted my prom days back—days when you could kiss a boy for twenty minutes in the back of a car and the windows would steam up, and sure, he'd break your heart eventually, but he'd actually make out with you before he tried to put his hands on your breasts or down your pants, and it was romantic. And, as

I crossed Houston, I was wishing my husband would kiss me for twenty minutes straight because, if he did, I knew I'd forgive him. I was sure my heart was about to rupture when the driver of that big old truck slammed on the brakes and blew the horn, the *M* of the Mack bigger than my head. I froze, then ran across the rest of the street. When I looked up to the driver to say thank you for sparing my life, he gave me the finger and said, *Watch where you're going, you crazy bitch!* and I said *I'm sorry Mister! Really, I'm sorry!* even though that bastard probably bought porn, wasting money that he could have otherwise brought home to his wife who was missing him despite what she knew, crossing a street, dazed and upset, in Detroit.

Tina and the Bruised Hearts

I've always been a cautious woman
so, though I've never bounced a check,
I have overdraft protection. Because of this,
my ex is able to take money out of our account
long after it's empty. The irony is
I have to pay the money back plus a $49 fee
for each of his ATM withdrawals.
Shirlene, I say to a nametag, *please, you've got to
help me close this account.* Shirlene says
she'll need my ex's signature. I tell her
he's in Europe. She's sorry for me,
but that's just the way it is. *Shirlene,*
I plead, *has a man ever done you wrong?*
Tina, I beg the next teller, *what am I going to do?*
Tina says we can get rid of the overdraft protection,
but we'll need his signature for that, too. *Tina,*
has anyone ever taken your trust and snapped it like a twig?
When the other customers ask me, *What's the matter?*
I realize I'm sobbing and hunched
near a coffee machine with Styrofoam cups
and powdered creamer. I'm led to an office
where Shirlene and Tina can speak freely.
They both have had a man disappear
and take their faith and confidence with him.
He did _what_? they ask me. I sputter more of my story
as Shirlene whispers, *Look, that s.o.b. just
took out another five hundred bucks.*
Tina stands behind Shirlene, hovering
over the screen. *Goddamn!* Tina says, *You're right.*
It looks like he's in Amsterdam. What time is it over there?
Shirlene deactivates the account, the numbers

unscrambling like a bad marriage. For a moment,
we become a girl group, Tina and the Bruised
Hearts. My lawyer says I should put a fraud alert
on myself so my ex can't open any new joint accounts.
That works except now I can't get a phone in my name
without a hefty deposit to prove I'm really me.
You can't blame AT&T—
Tina, Shirlene, and I are almost indistinguishable
as we step up to harmonize in our hot pink hologram lamé.

Takeout, 2008

My sister, my brother-in-law, and I order Chinese takeout
on New Year's Eve and my fortune reads
"You have to accept loss to win." This makes me almost hopeful—
and maybe, for a moment, even gives me a way
to make sense out of 2008. *I am going to keep that fortune,* I think,
but then promptly, accidentally, I throw it in the trash.
Later my sister says that she thought my fortune might have read,
"Only through learning to lose can you really win."
Or "Maybe accepting loss makes you a winner." I can't search
through the trash because I threw the bag of leftover Chinese
into the condo's chute, which crushes whatever thuds to the bottom.
Yesterday I held my childhood drawings in my hand
except they had been drenched in sewer water, so it's more accurate to say
that I scooped Crayola pulp in my work gloves. The apartment
my sister and brother-in-law and I bought is gone, except
for the cement floor. Even the moldy walls must come down.
My sister and I hauled away the kitchen sink.
My brother-in-law wore a mask and a white Tyvek suit, prying up
the wet tiles with a screwdriver. The cabinets, the mattress,
the couch, the loveseat all gone. The books too wavy and stinky to keep.
My teenage diaries and early poems, inky mush. Everything
down the chute. I had stored my old papers in the new apartment
so my husband could have more room. My father died
the Tuesday before Thanksgiving, my apartment flooded
on Christmas—and did I mention my husband left me
September 10th? One of the reasons we bought the extra apartment
in July of 2008 was so my beloved would have a place
where he could make his art. When he left
it wasn't a civil "I've had enough . . ." departure. No.
There were suicide notes. There were threats.
He was even a missing person for a while, a danger to himself
and others, as the police wrote down on their forms. Oh, Elizabeth

Bishop, loss *is* hard to master, if you ask me. Good-bye, good-bye,
my dear papa. We bought the apartment because I thought my parents
could come down to Florida for a month in the winter to escape the cold.
The psychic said my father would do just fine in the operation
and he'd be calling me Skipper and walking with me on the beach
by March. The psychic said, *Don't worry, your husband will never bring you harm.*
She told me to sage my apartment to keep safe. She said,
You are attached to your husband by a cord running from your stomach to his.
Every night I want you to work on loosening that cord before you fall asleep, OK?
After a few weeks of working on letting him go, I gave a slight tug
and he floated away. I whispered, *Good-bye, my love. Take care.*
Then that very night I dreamt he was back lying on the yellow couch
and I was yelling at him to get up and get a job. So many people tried
to help me this year—the pregnant clerk in Walmart who said,
If you give in to your anger, you give away your power . . .
my students, who drove me to the supermarket and the chiropractor
when my crumpled car was in the shop, and even the woman
whose car I wrecked on the way to the divorce lawyer
who said, *It's OK, it's OK, no one's hurt.*
Did I tell you that the poetry class I was supposed to teach was cancelled?
Did I tell you I smashed my toenail with the wet-vac and it really hurts?
Did I tell you I lost $200 in the time it took me to get from the ATM
back into the Honda? Did I tell you that I dropped the $320
I clutched in a roll either in CVS or the post office?
That I retraced my steps, but the clerks just laughed at my panic?
Did I tell you that this year I have gotten on my knees
and prayed for grace and peace of mind to get through the next hour?
I know there are people with missing children, not missing husbands.
I had my father 47 long years. There are people without a place
to sleep tonight. I know that. My mother asks me
to please turn off the TV as she doesn't want to watch the CNN story
about the terrorist attacks in India on the day of my father's wake.

After the surgeons worked fourteen hours on my dad,
he was so full of fluids they couldn't close him back up.
I wasn't there because I thought everything was going
to be all right (not only because of the psychic, but because of a feeling I had
that nothing else could go wrong this year). I was into being positive
and strong—lighting white candles, holding the thought of my dad
on his favorite recliner, buying him special vitamins to help him
heal faster after his heart valve replacement. My father was oozing fluids
at the end and cried pink tears, which were probably saline tinged with blood.
My brother-in-law pulled the sheet over his face. I want to pull the sheet
over this poem, over this entire year. I wasn't in the hospital
because I was teaching a class—not the one that had been cancelled,
but a fiction class the university asked me to do instead. I had wanted
to sit in on a fellow professor's graduate plot class because I want to write
fiction, too. But the undergrad fiction class I was asked to teach
was on the same night. I had already missed two weeks of classes
because of my husband's disappearance, so my work ethic (passed on
from my dad) made me stay in Florida instead of going to Rhode Island
to be with him the day of his operation. The doctor said to me,
Your heartbeat is double what it should be, but the good news is
you've lost 20 pounds. If you keep this up, Meryl Streep can play you
in the TV movie. He was making fun of my life—my list of complaints
that I rattled off so quickly they probably sounded made up.
Even my therapist has started to look at me with suspicion.
She knows she dare not ask, *What do you think you're getting out of all this crisis?*
I skip the New Year's Eve party because my sister and her husband
tried to fly home this morning, but their plane couldn't land
in the Providence snow and they were rerouted back.
Ten hours later they landed in the very same place
I drove them to this morning. I remade the futon
and hung up the towels I'd just washed and put away.
There can be no movie of my life at the moment unless someone else

writes it—I never did sit in that class and get the hang of plot,
though I am learning on my own about reversals.
What does the main character (me) want? Does she ever get it?
What are the obstacles in her way? My sister and her husband
are falling asleep before the ball drops, before the fireworks,
the sounds of which have always made me afraid. It is already 2009
in Bangkok, where 61 partygoers were killed in nightclub fire.
The party was billed on the poster as a "blowout." Yes,
there are people far worse off than I. My husband used to caress my hairline
to help me sleep, but tonight I'll take another Xanax. My sister says,
Please go out with your friends. We'll be fine. I skip the party
because it's hard on this last day of this year to yuck it up and laugh.
And the only other alternative is to go and be a drag. I am trying
to be more like Elizabeth Bishop. I am trying to remember the exact wording
of my fortune, though my friend told me last week that stress
erodes one's memory and stress-eroded memory never comes back.
Oh no, I said. She looked confused, explaining she didn't tell me to upset me,
only so that I would try harder to de-stress. I keep hearing the hum
of the industrial fans and the wet-vac. Another friend said, *Look!*
There's this article in the New Yorker *about someone else*
who just wrote a book of poetry about money. He cut it out for me
and everything. The poet is Katy Lederer. The article is called
"The Ballad of the Bubble." *Shit,* I said, *just my luck.* And my friend said,
I didn't tell you to depress you—I told you to show you how you were in the zeitgeist.
My new book coming out in February is called *Ka-Ching!,*
a word that can mean either a windfall or a big loss.
My friend called my beloved the Bear Stearns of Husbands because he melted down
at the same time as the investment firm. My sister and her husband
are going to try to get on that same plane again in the morning.
I set my alarm for 5 a.m. so I can drive them to the airport.
I wonder if Meryl Streep can do my Rhode Island accent.
I wonder if they'll give her a frizzy wig. It is already 2009

in London where takeout is called takeaway—and I say, take away 2008.
Out, out, out, long wretched year! Year with an excruciating "leap second"
added to keep the world's clocks on time with the globe's slowing rotation.
When I taught fiction this fall, I kept talking about the sympathetic narrator,
since some of my students kept picking jerks to tell their stories.
And sometimes I suspected the jerky narrator was a lot like the student
writing the piece. I am a lot like the narrator of this poem—
I am, in fact, completely her. I always tried to be tactful when I said in class
that the average reader might not care about this particular narrator's plight.
So I don't blame you, dear reader, for not caring about mine either.
I will try to be more likeable in my next poem.
For now, I'm broke and alone. A Dolly Parton song.
Still, I am trying harder, faster. Still, I am trying to learn the art.

Ritual

At two a.m. I unlocked our wedding picture from its silver frame and headed to the ocean. I packed a flashlight and a box of matches, but the wind would not let me burn our marriage away. No matter how I positioned our bodies or tried to block us from a brewing tropical storm, his side of the picture wouldn't catch fire. His stubborn cummerbund, his bowtie. I tried to set myself in flames. My veil, my fake crystal earrings. The picture was dampening in my hands.

I dug a hole and forced us into it. His tiny sideburns, my garish bouquet. Our interlocked hands crumpling. His gold band, my white fingernails. Even in the sand pit, each flint tip burned out. I finally tore us and flung the pieces like a collage into the waves. I hoped the shreds would travel from Florida to the Spanish coast where I guessed he was. A soggy nose, a coattail, a train. But we kept washing up, tiny limp jellyfish at my feet.

He and I were ready to end, but I needed a ritual to make it so. Something to replace the black empty rectangle on the bureau. Something to replace his empty drawers.

Recession Commandments

FORECLOSURE

thou shalt not covet thy neighbor's house
thou shalt not covet thy neighbor's corner lot nor thy neighbor's broadband connection
nor granite countertops nor thy neighbor's ease in large groups of people
 nor thy neighbor's two-car garage nor pool nor marble tile nor screened-in porch
 nor thy neighbor's healthy eating habits nor closet space nor billiard room
 nor central air nor salt-and-pepper shakers nor thy neighbor's direct sunlight
thou shalt not covet thy neighbor's wife nor garden nor gardener nor Lexus
 nor thy neighbor's perfect children nor thy neighbor's popularity
 nor clean driving record nor thy neighbor's husband and his sweet job
 nor thy neighbor's credit score nor vacation plans nor thy neighbor's wardrobe
 nor washing machine nor friendly hello's nor energy nor energy drinks
 nor hair-styling products nor kayak nor spice rack nor thy neighbor's Jacuzzi
thou shalt not covet thy neighbor's Merry Maids nor contractors nor pedigree dogs
 nor thy neighbor's manicures nor thy neighbor's spa memberships
 nor backscratcher nor matching luggage nor table manners nor graceful walk
 nor thy neighbor's passport nor trust fund nor safe full of cash nor curtains
 nor down comforter nor leather couch nor thy neighbor's charity work
thou shalt not covet thy neighbor's oxygen bar nor ass nor Assembly of God membership
 nor anything else that is thy neighbor's—not tennis rackets nor rollerblades
 nor art collection nor wine glasses nor Costco membership nor ice cubes
 nor commanding presence in a room nor junk mail and catalogs
 nor flawless articulation nor perfect posture nor political connections nor gutters
 nor scrapbook nor table runner nor encyclopedias nor vintage postcards
 nor brand new hammer nor chopsticks nor straight white teeth nor snow globe
 nor banister nor microwavable popcorn nor private jokes nor flirtatiousness
 nor TVs nor sound system nor shoe collection nor recessed lighting
 nor magazine subscriptions nor umbrellas nor umbrella stand nor sense of humor
 nor king size bed nor Sunday afternoon bicycle rides to get fresh air

UNEMPLOYMENT

for six days thou shalt labor and do all thy work
for six days thou shalt post thy resume, hand deliver thy resume, rewrite thy resume
      to best suit labor sought, mail thy resume overnight or priority, fudge thy resume
for six days thou shalt kept track of all thy efforts to qualify for an extension
      of unemployment benefits
for six days thou shalt feel guilty, cry, wring thy hands, redo thy checkbook,
      pawn thy TV and thy jewelry
for six days thou shalt fill out applications at chain restaurants, hospitals, retail stores,
      schools, offices of all types (including temp offices), banks, nail salons, hair salons,
      supermarkets, nursing homes, construction sites, topless bars, hotdog stands
for six days thou shalt set up an e-bay account to sell thy dishes, and thou shalt bring
      thy best clothes to a consignment shop
for six days thou shalt call up favors and let go of thy pride
for six days thou shalt apply for no-interest credit cards
for six days thou shalt fill out applications to become a telemarketer, a customer
      service employee, a tutor, a nanny, a janitor, a maid, a dog-walker,
      a dogcatcher, a cashier, a mail order bride
for six days thou shalt write letters to government officials when unemployment
      extension benefits are denied
for six days thou shalt labor and do all the work thou can find

INFLATION

thou shalt watch *American Idol*, whether on TV or podcast
      thou shalt watch anything that will give thee false hope—that thou could compete
      on a show like America Has Talent or I Love Money to earn a windfall,
      that thou could once again afford Heavenly Hash ice cream, Earth shoes,
      or a new Brita water filter
thou shalt not even dare window-shop for a killer purse, adult DVDs, sunglasses
      that last year thou would have thought a bargain

thou shalt ignore the news—the Pacific Island nation of Palau threatened
    with disappearance; houses in Shishmaref, Alaska, plunging into the sea;
    a redrawn map of the United States with Florida (where thou livest)
    chopped off, submerged
thou shalt not relive the hurricanes, especially Katrina, after which thou bought gas
    cards and boxed up all the little toiletries, shampoos and soaps, thou had taken
    (though thou shalt not steal) from hotels, to send to New Orleans
    because even people who lost everything might want to smell good
    and rub a little lotion into their arms
thou shalt not buy too much gas, thou shalt not go too far, thou shalt not replace
    the stove nor the lightbulb nor the shoelaces nor the baking soda in the fridge
thou shalt not be nostalgic
thou shalt not bear witness to the sad stories around thee—the abandoned hotels,
    once swanky, but now full of crack; the girl squatting in an apartment
    with nothing but a mattress and a webcam; the man living in his car,
    washing in the outdoor showers at the beach before he heads off to work
thou shalt not believe it, thou shalt not inflate thine own suffering
    nor the suffering of others
thou shalt not believe it could happen to thee

Heartburn

I put in the movie, then start dipping
breadsticks into a container of hummus,
my dinner, as I watch
Meryl Streep and Jack Nicholson
their first night together, scarfing the pasta
she's made at 4 a.m. They're in her bed,
twirling their forks into the same big bowl
just like the scene in *An Unmarried Woman*
in which Jill Clayburgh and Alan Bates
gobble her famous omelet with Tabasco sauce
from the same skillet.
I have never eaten anything
with anyone from the same pot
or serving dish. Maybe I have missed out
by not learning to cook
something simple and sexy
to offer in a postcoital
moment. I have spent
a good part of my life afraid
of food and men, one of whom
asked, *Why is there only Diet Coke
and a head of cabbage in your fridge?* It's true
that I've rented *She-Devil, War of the Roses,*
and *The First Wives Club* on DVD,
but I still haven't found the divorce
movie that truly captures
my situation. I am much happier
than when I was married,
but as Meryl Streep's shrink
(Maureen Stapleton) tells her,
"Divorce is only a temporary solution."
No one gets heartburn in *Heartburn,*

which makes the title too much
of a pun, in my opinion. Still,
I can relate to the shouting matches,
the ransacking of pockets and drawers,
looking for clues. After my husband
left, I found dozens and dozens
of Alka-Seltzer packets he'd bought
for an art project. He'd written
words on the tablets with a Sharpie,
then dropped them into water,
filming them as they fizzled
and disappeared. I find his YouTube video
and watch as I eat dessert. I have to admit
he had some good ideas.

An Unmarried Woman

When I first saw it, I was a high school junior. Clayburgh was scandalous
dancing ballet in her tee shirt and panties, showing her teenage daughter
a wet spot on the bed after she'd made love to her husband, the girl's father.

I was fascinated by her lip gloss and feathered hair.
I had a Fair Isle sweater just like hers and wanted the crazy cape
in which she wraps her new lover on a cobblestone street in New York.

I didn't understand then, of course, that I would someday be divorced
after sixteen years of marriage, just like her character, throwing up
on a sidewalk just like she did, jittery in a therapist's office,

having an awful blind date, eating dim sum with a stranger
who would try to kiss her in a cab. Instead of pirouetting
to *Swan Lake,* I jumped around the apartment, singing

along with Beyoncé and Pink. Back then, in 1978, I didn't quite get
the point. I just liked Jill's outfits—the skirt and tank in the final scene
that reminds me now of Sarah Jessica Parker's ensemble in the opening credits

of *Sex and the City.* When her artist-lover gives Jill a giant painting
as he heads off to Vermont for the summer, and she carries it through Soho,
fumbling and twisting in the wind, you can't help but root for Jill,

just as I am rooting for myself, watching this movie again on DVD
thirty years later, part of my postdivorce Netflix recovery.
Jill, today, is in the obituaries. Breast cancer, chronic lymphocytic leukemia—

how can that be? She looks so young and fresh as she ice-skates
with her pals, runs along the East River where her husband steps in dog shit
and blames her. When I first saw *An Unmarried Woman,* I went with my friend

and, if I remember correctly, we were freaked out by the sex scenes
and barely acknowledged Jill's bland teenage daughter
who would have been about our age. Afterward, at Friendly's, we talked

about the pickled herring arc. Jill's lover tells the story
about how his mother threw a jar toward his father's head
and how, as he watched the fish smash against the wall, he decided

to become an abstract painter. Toward the end of the movie,
the lover himself lobs a jar at Jill when she doesn't do what he wants.
My friend told me her mother hurled a bottle of applesauce at her father

and when she missed, the stuff ruined the wallpaper.
That was just marriage, we guessed, sipping our frappes.
We put our hands over our hearts and pledged we'd never wed

even as the cute boys came in, crowding into a booth
across from us. We blushed and giggled despite ourselves.
Adults, we agreed, were crazy—we wanted no part of their messes.

Two

Kindergarten Boyfriend

My kindergarten boyfriend
said his mother had taught him to waltz,
so I told my mother about how he'd taught me,
how we glided around the schoolyard during recess.
How all the other kids dropped their balls
and abandoned their jump romps to watch us.
My mother said, *Really?* like she didn't believe me,
which made me angry even though my story
was totally untrue. I liked to color with the boy,
who was quiet like I was. One day, after biting
into a cracker, he spat out his front tooth,
which looked like a tiny ice cube
on the pad of his finger. The teacher
made a fuss and wrapped his tooth in tissue.
During naptime, he slept on a plastic mat by my side.
I stayed awake trying to will him to give the tooth to me,
but when I asked him his plans, he told me
he was going to take it home to put under his pillow.
I flung puzzle pieces and started to cry.
Even then, my expectations were too high.

Fourth Grade Boyfriend

In fourth grade, the fattest boy in class wrote me a love letter
that read, *Welcome to this new school.*
You are very pretty. I want to be your boyfriend. I didn't like his plaid shirt
or his big melon head, so I crumpled up the note and ignored him.
Soon though I realized how hard it was to be the new girl
when the other girls had sleepovers to which I wasn't invited
and the other boys were mean and spit in the water fountain.
A few weeks later I wrote back, *Sorry it's taken me so long to answer.*
OK. I'll be your girlfriend. He walked me home, showing me the shortcut
through the woods, the "umbrella graveyard" where kids abandoned
anything they were too ashamed to carry—out-of-date
lunchboxes, shirts and coats no longer in style. Umbrellas,
which, he explained, were uncool, no matter what.
Sometimes a girl would change shoes on the path,
leaving the ugly ones she had to wear at home hanging
from their laces on a branch. The fat boy huffed and puffed
up the tiniest inclines. I did too—it was fall
and that's when my asthma flared up. One time my nose started to bleed
and, because I didn't have any tissues, the fat boy gave me
his science worksheet, then a big maple leaf, to catch the blood.
So what if he couldn't dance? That was love.

My Shortcut

the summer I was ten the teenage boys next door
stole my panties from the clothesline
my mother knew it was them
their dirty car with their blistering music
they skinny-dipped with girls in their pool
while their parents were on vacation
I heard splashes once in the middle of the night
and peeked from my window to see
their slick dolphin bodies their patches of hair
as they took turns doing cannonballs diving

that September the boys' father
wouldn't let me cut through his yard anymore
which was my shortcut to school
rabbits had come to take a bite out of each of his tomatoes
but he blamed the neighborhood kids
though we all hated vegetables
and would never have bent to chomp
the warm beefsteaks that hung on his vine
go around he snapped aiming the hose at us
I want my underpants back

I wanted to say but didn't
instead I wondered about what kind of rabbit
or gopher or groundhog would be so fussy or curious
as to sample each tomato and move on to the next
the way a kid might take a bite from each chocolate
in a fancy box to test the filling inside
it would take Anne Marie and me
a good ten minutes longer to get to fifth grade
since we had to walk on sidewalks now
and wait for traffic guards to get us across streets

one morning the teenage brothers pulled up
turning down their Jimi Hendrix cassette
the one who was driving said *hop in we'll give you a ride*
I was tempted by the cracked leather seat
with orange foam swelling through
our old man's crazy the other brother said
he's obsessed with his garden I'd never really talked
to teenagers before except my cousins who were forced
to play board games with me at Christmas
I felt seriously grown-up as I reached

for the loose rusty door handle
at first I pretended not to hear
when Anne Marie called to me that we'd be late
her first-grade sister loping behind
but then Pam smiled flashed me
her missing-tooth smile
there was the same blank space on the clothesline
where my panties had been snatched
so I ran toward the sisters
Anne Marie tapping the face of her Bobby Sherman watch

Lower East Side Boyfriend

When I came home from work, I saw a package for him,
so I took it up to the sixth floor where he lived.
I was panting a bit since I wasn't used to the climb.
I lived on the second floor of the same building
with busted mailboxes and marble steps, worn thin
toward the side nearer the banister from all those years
of people ascending and descending—the immigrants first,
then the working poor, and now drug addicts and artists.
There was no doorman, and in place of our buzzer,
just a few dangling red wires. The mailman dumped
packages and magazines onto the floor
of our phone booth–sized foyer. The second metal door
had a square of mesh over the glass window
because someone had smashed it in.
Everything was painted a spooky gray,
and the halls smelled like must and mold.
Most of the blue and cream tiles
that I imagined were once beautiful
were broken or missing. The maintenance man
my roommate called "a junkie with a hammer"
had put some pink putty that looked like old bubblegum
in places where the tile was completely gone.
I was curious about the man who subscribed
to *Art Forum* and *Spy* and *Time,* all of which
I had been stepping over in the foyer.
His FedEx box was heavy in my arms
as I climbed those eroded warped stairs,
which were hard to negotiate, like walking
on a beach, one foot in the water,
the other on an incline in wet sand.
There was an occasional crack vial on a landing

that I'd kick into a corner. When he opened the door
he was just like the neighborhood, tragic
and ravished and exquisite. He was holding
his arm in a bunch of bloody paper towels.
He'd just put his fist through a glass coffee table
at his girlfriend's place—she lived
a few blocks north and west. They'd had a fight,
and he was picking out translucent slivers
from his arm. I wondered if he'd also smashed the glass
on the metal security door. When I knocked,
he probably thought I was the girlfriend,
begging to take him back. I looked over his shoulder
at the mattress on the floor, the tiny refrigerator
like college kids have in dorms. As he told me
his troubles, they seemed to drift into the past,
and I knew that I'd be his next girlfriend.
He was forty and I was twenty-eight, a little out of breath
from the stairs, a little beyond grad school, but not much.
A poet, I said. *A painter,* he said. *I've lived here two years,* I said.
Eighteen years for me. He had the old kind of apartment
that was not yet renovated, a toilet in the hall
that he shared with two other bachelors on his floor.
A filthy bowl that no one bothered to clean,
a dusty lightbulb with a chain, a defunct lock
that looked as though, at one point, it might have been
accessed by a skeleton key. I went into his apartment
and sat on his mattress, as there were no chairs
or couch. He said, *You want a drink?* His walls were blank.
I contemplated asking where all his paintings were,
but instead I took the tweezers from his shaking hand
and began to pull out the shards from his palm.

36

The Widow

She dove to a deep place
on the bottom of the black ocean
below the anemonefish and coral reefs. She tries to explain

where she's been, her pink lipstick smearing, as we eat
peel-and-eat shrimp. She holds on
to her compact and pain and the memoir she started five days ago

and her two cats and her roommate and her sanctuary
and her wedding ring she threw in the grate after his death
and the new fake wedding ring she bought

to replace it. Widow, window, wind, wide world, Windex.
There are some things you can't wash away, some smudges
that stay on the glass no matter how hard you scrub.

My favorite lipstick is Revlon #90, Bali brown.
I wore it for six years and then it became hard to find,
so whenever I saw it at a drugstore, I would buy two.

And then, last year, it was just completely gone.
Women always asked, *Where did you get that lipstick?*
It's perfect for your coloring. I kept trying to match it

and bought about six other lipsticks—too dark,
too bronzy, too matte, until I found one I could live with,
though for me it was a little too pink.

It was the kind of lipstick that would have looked good
on the widow, the poet-mermaid with glossy black hair
whose tragedy was all the worse

because she had been lucky
to find the love she found. I finally unearthed
a tube of Revlon Bali-brown lipstick

on eBay—it was discontinued, twice the price
of what I originally paid, but I kept bidding—
I couldn't help it. My chance to recapture

what I thought was gone forever. I am careful now
about how often I reapply, knowing I'm only postponing
the eventual concave grave.

Loaded

This morning on CNN I see a white hamster
lounge between two black piano keys.
The hamster's gnawing away
on popcorn, its paws holding a kernel
that it twists like corn on the cob.
Everything seems out of proportion,
the giant kernel, the tiny rodent.
I think about my failed marriage,
how my ex hopped off the wheel
while I kept running. How he loaded up
a suitcase and left me with all our debt
and creditors looking for him to pay his bills.
The hamster lazes on its back, lifting
its hind legs in what seems like pure bliss.
I imagine my ex, who has been gone
for a while now, living like this
on the money I gave him in our settlement.
When he first went missing,
I kept seeing a mouse run across the wall,
so I set out traps, globbed
with peanut butter my ex had left behind.
Every morning I checked, sure I'd find
some awful dead thing, but the traps
were empty. It took me a few days to realize
the mouse I thought I'd seen was the shadow
of a bird who flew above the balcony outside.
Once again I was wrong. Once again I saw
something that wasn't there and missed
the obvious. *Look how cute!*
The CNN announcer coos about the hamster,
today's YouTube sensation.
As I leave for work, I say, *By the way, I hate you,*

to the pampered hamster, who is playing
on a loop, on every channel,
serenaded by big well-meaning hands.

Cleopatra Invented the First Vibrator

which was either a papyrus tube,
the rind of a calabash,
or a hollowed-out stone,
any of which was filled with buzzing bees.
I look back to my childhood projects,
the ants and spiders I'd hoped to cultivate
in jars, and wonder how she did it.
Even with crackers for food and air holes
punched into the lid, the insects always died
within a few hours of capture. If the bees
in Cleopatra's bottle gourd vibrator
got inside, couldn't they also get out?
And if they were sealed in without ventilation,
wouldn't they have perished, the equivalent
of dead Duracells? Some conjecture Cleopatra
coaxed the workers directly to her vulva, stimulated
by the stinging. But I think not—her tears
would have turned the kohl around her eyes to mud.
More accurately recorded was her beauty routine—
everyone agrees she kept her skin supple with honey.

My New Chum

is still in her dressing gown
when I ring her on her mobile.
Blimey! So sorry. I'm running late.
Give me a few minutes to get my lippy on.
I'm still slap-free, she says. *I've got to grab*
my bum bag and jumper. She asks me
if I've packed my swimming costume.
We are going to the sea for a chin wag.
I hope she fancies the scrummy snacks
I've packed, especially the squidgy cake.
She runs down the stairs, full of beans.
Pip pip! she calls out to her husband.
Cheerio, he waves. She is from Surrey
and I am from the States.
She's bought me a book: *English for Americans.*
Our friendship is tickety-boo, though she hates
Austin Powers and George Bush.
She doesn't mean to be a whinger,
but she can't get over the porkies
that got us into Iraq, the whole shambolic mess.
She's been married five years, and everything
was pukka at first—their easy peasy rumpy pumpy,
his luvvly-jubbly humming. But now he's bloody
blinkered when it comes to trying anything new.
He can't be fagged to take the rubbish to the skip.
To tell you the truth, we've just had a stonking row.
I unwrap the cake to cheer her up.
Ooh, it's mutt's nuts! she squeals, taking a bite.
She grabs her belly, *But this can't be good for my muffin top!*
As I pour her a cup of fizzy water, I tell her
I get frustrated too, when my husband sits all day
in front of the boob tube. My new chum laughs.

For her, a "boob tube" is a bra, "knickers" underpants.
At least your husband doesn't throw wobblers, she says.
Mine constantly has a strop on. They met in uni.
He was ace, brill, a real cheeky monkey.
I was gobsmacked in love. Crikey! Now he's always taking
a kip on the couch, after tracking up the house
in his beastly muddy trainers. Her eyes catch the eyes
of a dishy bloke walking toward the parking lot.
No! I say, pulling her hand, yanking her up
from our blanket. *I'm only having a dekko,* she protests.

We run to the surf, and I try to assure her
that her nuptials weren't a complete cock-up.
Don't be daft, I'm miserable, she says, *just like you.*
Chips or crisps, two weeks or a fortnight—it's all the same
as I try to pass off codswallop as jolly good advice.
We splash until we are lobsters, until she makes me
admit marriage takes the biscuit. Then
her holiday ends. She'll email me soon
that she's ditched her wasband. *Ta,* she says.
Bob's your uncle! Best of British!

A Different Story

The day after I'd written a poem about her,
my new friend asks if I sometimes steal stories
from other people's lives. She doesn't know
many poets, but she once met a woman
who wrote self-help books about dating.
We're at a diner, where great stories
are often exchanged. The writer utilized
my new friend's tale of woe but made it even worse,
more embarrassing than it actually was.
I say writers are always stealing, we can't
help ourselves, and she says she understands
though it gives her the creeps. I don't confess
my own theft but instead tell her about a poet
whose ex writes thrillers. One of his recent characters
has her name, her physical traits, and her most
unflattering of habits. Worst of all, the character
is stabbed to death in the final chapter.
Writers must have a lot of issues, my new friend says, lifting
the limp pickles off the pale inside of her hamburger bun.
We both fall silent. She eyes me suspiciously
as she salts her fries. I stop asking her about her past,
about her day, fearing she'll tell me something so good
I'll be tempted to take it for another poem. Our Diet Cokes
are almost drained when she wonders if the poet,
having suffered her own fictional fatality,
has changed her ways, has stopped using her friends
as subject matter. *Imagine how you'd feel
if someone re-created your life and it wasn't very pretty.*
I start to write the poem in my head, the one
describing my blubber, my crowded teeth, my penchant
for gossip, the smell of my feet after a long day

in plastic sandals. My character is cheap,
fearful, controlling, duplicitous, a dunce.
Want to split a slice of pie? I think she says,
but I am already slapping a twenty
on the Formica table, sliding out of the booth.
I have to get it all down before someone else does.

You're Looking at the Love Interest

It's a long story, but basically
I'm stuck in Lincoln, Nebraska, and need to get to Omaha
to catch my flight back to Fort Lauderdale.
The person who is supposed to pick me up
has overslept. When he doesn't answer his cell phone,
I call the local cab company that can't let its cars
leave Lincoln because of some law that takes
the person answering too long to explain. The next hotel shuttle
departs an hour from now and I will miss my flight
if I wait for it. The woman behind the desk says,
There's one more option—a car service—but it'll cost you.
I negotiate a price—$200 for an hour's ride—and run
to the nearest ATM. I'm expecting a town car,
but a driver arrives in a pickup truck. I climb in
and the usual chitchat begins except I keep pressing him—
will I make my plane? *You sure will,* he says,
I used to drive this route all the time. Why was I in Omaha?
To give a lecture, I say.
A lecture about what? the driver asks.
I confess that I'm a poet.
Oh, so you read last night. You must be Denise.
My ex-wife was there. She's a poet, too.
He describes her to me: long gray hair, red sweater.
She had the first question at the Q&A. *What about Ted Kooser?* he says.
Do you like his work? Yes! The driver's favorite book of his:
Weather Central. We talk Nebraska poets: Hilda Raz, Weldon Kees.
The benefits of living here: cheap rent, good air.
His favorite writer of all time? Arthur Miller.
It's a long shot, I say, *but do you know Meghan Daum?*
Before I tell him she writes prose,

his grin fills the rearview mirror.
Know her? he beams. *You're looking at the love interest!*
I ask, *You mean from* The Quality of Life Report?
He confirms he's indeed that guy. *But aren't you*
supposed to be a carpenter? That's what you are in her book.
He says Meghan has since talked him into taking work
on the side as a driver since he brought her back and forth
to the airport so many times. *Besides, that's a novel,* he explains.
He assures me he's only 70 percent as bad
as she made him out to be and tells me,
scene by scene, his version of the story.
But, hey, no hard feelings—he says he understands
why Meghan had to make him out to be a little bit of a jerk.
No conflict, no story, right? As long as he came across
as a sexy guy in the book, what the heck. *I mean,*
the ex in your poems probably isn't as terrible
as he is on the page, he says, sliding into
the passenger drop-off zone and hoisting my bag
to the curb. I wonder if he's trying to tell me his ex-wife, the poet,
has written about him too. I'll stay married two more years,
before my ex becomes the villain in my villanelle.
Run, the love interest says. *You're going to make it.*
He checks the extra crumpled bills I put in his hand.
And his tip to me: *Betrayal is the only truth that sticks.*

Or Wherever Your Final Destination May Be

The spring before my husband left me, I sat next to a flirt on the plane. He was a businessman, kind of cute, with curly black hair. I did my best to flirt back. I was so unused to aggressive men that, though I was flattered, I cringed a bit, too.

"Your voice is so sexy," he said.

"What?"

"I mean, you end each sentence by lowering your voice."

I realized I was not being myself—I usually ended each sentence in a question. People pointed it out all the time.

I didn't reply because I was self-conscious.

I was coming home from a poetry conference. I was sitting on the left side of the plane—there were only two seats in our row.

"So when did you get divorced?" he asked.

"I'm happily married," I lied.

"Sure you are," he said.

"I am." My voice was suddenly squeaky and high.

"You compartmentalize," he said.

He hadn't seemed interested when I told him I was a poet. He told me that in his job he had to know how to sum up people. He drew squares on his JetBlue napkin. "Here is your brain; here is your heart, and here is your sex drive." The latter was the biggest square.

I felt myself get wet, which hadn't happened in a very long time. I thought I never would again because of my age.

"You're a jerk," I said.

"Whatever." He leaned over to me and whispered, "But I'd still like to take you to my hotel and fuck you."

I wanted to take his hand and put it between my legs. I wished I were wearing a skirt instead of jeans.

"I'm going to ask to be moved to a different seat," I snapped.

"No, you're not."

I tried to look as much like a stone as possible. I kept my eyes in my lap, wishing I had a book or magazine. We sat in silence for a long time until I finally fished out my headphones and clumsily plugged them into the armrest between us so I could watch the TV. I stared at CNN and soon I heard the flirt snoring.

I turned to him in his window seat. He was more ugly than I originally thought. His shirt was polyester not cotton. Probably middle management. I was middle-aged. This was my future, I thought, if I left my husband. I didn't know then that my husband had plans of his own.

The flight attendant came by to pick up our cups. I shoved the flirt's napkin, his sloppily drawn squares, into the trash bag she held out.

The stranger didn't wake up until touchdown when a young woman's voice on the speaker wished us a safe trip in Fort Lauderdale or wherever our final destinations may be. The man gave me a big smile, as though we had spent the night together and he didn't regret it. His teeth were straight and white—he was the kind of man who, as a kid, wore braces.

I was the first to hop up and get my luggage from the overhead bin.

As my sleeves pulled, I felt my shirt rise. I wondered if the flirt could see a strip of my belly skin. For a second, I imagined his fingers reaching for my button, my zipper. He said something like I had one last chance. I said something like I had to get home to my husband. Then, without looking back, I pushed my way down the aisle—the metaphor not lost on me. The steward blessed each of us, *thank you and have a good evening*. I bolted to the taxi stand like a late bride.

Courtship

I used to write poems in one sitting while he slept.
I printed them out so he could read them
as soon as he woke up. He tried to write about my shoulder once—
I saw a few lines on the back blank cover of my phonebook—
but he never finished. Or maybe it wasn't my shoulder?
I was threatened by his friendship with Donna.
Once he spent a whole day shopping with her
at Lancôme and Clinique counters,
helping her pick out which lipstick suited her best,
and described to me in detail the heels she tried on.
He didn't get why I thought that was sexual.
He was a sucker for a pretty face (not always mine)
and it's a miracle that we even got married
because though he was sweet, he fucked up a lot in those days.
And though I was sweet, I was basically a lunatic.
One night he went out with his friend Howard at 6,
promising he'd bring me back dinner in about an hour.
He showed up past midnight—no food—and I was so angry
I couldn't speak. I had to work the next morning.
He was in grad school, so he could sleep in.
The spice rack smashed to the floor.
We were sure it was my anger that softened
the plaster and loosened the nails.
Curry powder splattered onto the six squares of linoleum
in my tiny studio kitchen and stained it yellow.
I stepped on glass slivers and rosemary twigs
until I moved out
so we could get married.

Worst Case Scenario

Your house washes away to sea. The whoosh is subliminal. You're terminal. It's totaled. They say you're a floozy. The trapeze comes loose. You're ten minutes late. He leaves you. He leaves you for someone else. He betrays you and begs you to stay. He dies. You dye it back to the original color. You move. You become a maven of rot. You sell the antique teapot. You can't stop the infection. He wins the election. Reconstructive surgery. You adopt. The child will adapt. You divorce. They use force. You get your cards replaced. Your mortgage balloons into a double bassoon. You start over. You overplay your hand. You wish you were dead. You get a new job. You steal food. Your bathtub crashes right through the moist floorboards and lands downstairs, demolishing your neighbor's bathroom. You move on. He won't let you take back what you said, no apology good enough. You use a voice-activated computer. You end up in prison. He ends up on parole. He makes his bail. You wear an eye patch to the mall. You try another brand. You up the dose. You take out the seams. Your trailer rooftop peels away like God is opening a can of Spam. Your insides get rained upon. Your haiku flops. You come in last place. You fall. You fail. You're too full to move. You look like a fool. You find out your winning was just a fluke. There's blood in your stool. Your car stalls at the light. Your mannerisms become stilted. You stand still. You become stale. You fall off your stilts. He slits his wrist. You make a fist. You get up too fast. You miss the feast. He foists himself on someone else. You end up in the state-run nursing home. You never grow up. Your hunger makes you queasy. You abandon your quest. They call you Quasimodo. You fail the quiz. You end up in showbiz. He kills your buzz. He becomes your boss. You go bust. You only make it to first base. Your blister pops. He calls the cops. You tip over your half-full cup. He flies the coop. His cap blows away. You get stuck in traffic trying to escape. You choke on a grape. You lose your grip. His hug becomes a grope. You get separated from the group. You stoop to his level. You don't see the stop sign. You trip on a step. You become a pest. You make a mess. The mouse is really a rat. The moose busts through the plate glass. They launch the missile while you sleep.

And So

And so it came to pass—
that on January 21, 2009, the day after
the inauguration, you came back
to pick up your stuff that I put in the middle
of the living room with a rope around it.
I'd left quarters on the table to feed the meter—
my last codependent gesture,
so your rental wouldn't get towed.
And so it came to pass—
that the first friend I called
after you disappeared 132 days ago
and his son, who helped me
set up a Facebook account so I could
try to talk you out of suicide,
met you to take away boxes
and bags and suitcases of your belongings
while I was lying in a hotel room
an hour north under a white comforter
with a mustard stain
I'd put there myself
eating a sandwich in bed the day before.
I couldn't eat today
as I thought of you in the apartment again.
My friend told me that you couldn't fit
everything into the Avis SUV, so you gave him
a couple of your antique typewriters
and a film projector and left me
with a few paintings to either keep
or throw away. *How did he look?*
I asked. Chubby, smoking a cigarette.
So I revised my joke—when people
asked how much weight I'd lost

I upped the punch line, "Two hundred
and eighty pounds. . . . Twenty of my own
plus my ex." I'm not sure how much
you really weighed, though you used to stand
on the scale when we first walked
into the supermarket like you were
a giant pineapple from produce.
You'd say, "Hey, I lost two pounds,"
or something like that. I would never
have weighed myself in public/Publix,
and I stood away, near the carriages,
to give you privacy. That's how freaked out
I was. I didn't want to monitor
your weight anymore
or the diabetes you ignored,
your glucose meter full of dust
when I crammed it between your sweatshirts
and socks in the suitcase.
I didn't want to monitor your porn
or your sleep habits or your blog.
And so it came to pass—
that while we were separated
Obama was elected.
I wept watching the first couple dance,
weeping with America,
weeping with relief,
but also weeping for us
because you were born the same year
as Michelle and I, the same year
as Barack, and we were married
the same year as they were
in the same church,

the United Church of Christ,
and what had we done
with our lives so far
except make a giant mess?
No Malia, no Sasha, no
hypoallergenic pup.
And so it came to pass—
you called me as you drove away
for the last time because you knew
I wasn't home. When I checked
my messages I heard you say—
hey, I got my stuff. Casual,
like it was no big deal.
It startled me to hear
your voice again. The police told me
when you vanished
in September that you'd call
within 24 hours
if you still were alive
and when that didn't happen
they admitted this was a very strange case.
When you started writing threats
and the police posted the safety alert,
they listed you as 5'10", two inches
taller than you actually were,
your weight listed as 260 pounds.
No one asked me for your statistics.
Could you really have weighed that much?
And so it came to pass—
that I slept again at last,
on the fourth day after you left.
Or rather, so it came to pass—

that I passed out, with my cell phone
in one hand and the cordless
in the other. And so it came to pass—
that today I waited for my friend
to call to give me an update,
to say you were quiet, mostly,
that it was a little weird, that you didn't ask
about me at all. And so it came to pass—
that you seemed, well,
happy, with your new GPS.
Happy like this mustard
stain, which looks like a sun poking
through clouds. What a coward,
I thought—calling when you knew
I wouldn't be home. What a brave soul,
I thought—driving north with
the gadget you'd always wanted
but I'd said no, since I was the one working
not you. And so it came to pass—
that the police asked me that first night
when you went missing
if we had such a device in my car,
the one that you stole, the one
that the police said you didn't really steal
since it was marital property.
Too bad you didn't buy that GPS for him, they said.
We could have traced him
to tell you exactly where he went.
And so it came to pass—finally,
that I didn't want to know.

Old Love Poems

I can burn the pictures, but not the poems
since I published them in books, which are on shelves
in libraries and in people's homes. Once my cousin told me
not to write anything down because the words would be there forever
to remind me of the fool I once was. My cousin
was the little dog on the Tarot card, barking at the Fool's heels
as I headed right toward the cliff.
                                        When James Taylor and Carly Simon
broke up, I was shocked. Taylor's drug use or not,
couldn't they work it out? I was in college
and, though I didn't really believe in marriage,
I believed in them. How could they part
having written those love songs? And how could they go on
singing those love songs after the divorce?
                                        But now, I know.
After time, when they reached for those notes,
there wasn't really a beloved there anymore,
just a strand of hair each left behind
on the other's scarf or pillow, a cologne trigger
more real than they were,
the lovers themselves ephemeral muses.
                                        It's still hard
for me to accept the notion of love outliving the lovers—
a notion so romantic, it's unromantic. Hard to accept
that those big lumps of affection
would find alternate places to stick,
that Simon and Taylor would be swept away and marry
others. That need is not so much a deficit
                                        as an asset,
like a wallet that keeps manufacturing its own dollar bills
even after it's been robbed of everything.
Or to say it another way: the plant that will bloom

despite being uprooted. The new seedling that will pop up.
It's hard to believe when you are down to your last penny,
when the soil is dry and rocky and full of weeds,

                                              when your love
is freeze-dried into a metallic pouch and you are full of snarky rage.
You look back at a love poem you wrote and ask:
did I really feel this way? Even if you no longer remember tenderness,
even if the verse was simply artifice, your idea of love, a subspecies
you made up to tag and define that one poor sap, you now read the poem
again, grateful, holding the words in your hands like a bunch of flowers.

Expired

When my mother says, *Take something of your father's to remember him by,*
I take his black and silver *D* cufflinks and an Albuterol inhaler—
the kind that comes in a white plastic tube, the kind
they don't make any more. The code on my father's inhaler has expired
but I don't care. My father put his lips to it
when he had trouble breathing. Albuterol didn't help
my father, but I knew it would help me
to put my mouth around it, to squeeze and breathe in something
he might have breathed himself. The inhalers they make now are more
"eco-friendly," but the squirt of Proventil isn't as forceful.
I like the old Albuterol, but it contained chlorofluorocarbons,
so the manufacturer stopped making it. I am all for the environment, of course,
since I'm asthmatic, yet these new inhalers in their yellow canisters
just don't have the oomph of the old ones. I am nostalgic,
just like my dad, who talked about the farm where he milked cows
in Canada. He never understood the appeal of skim milk
since that's what they used to give the pigs. He liked heavy cream
and whipped cream, too. Now everyone agrees
that skim milk is better for you than cream, that these new inhalers
are better than the old. The velocity of the puff is slower, making it easier
for the medicine to penetrate the lungs. At least that's what my doctor says.
But I miss that blast in the throat, that fast relief, the way I miss cream
when I'm trying to diet. The doctor tells me that honest, the medicine
in this new inhaler is the same, that it's just hard sometimes
to get used to change. I am using my dad's inhaler until it runs out,
until I absolutely have to say good-bye.

Three

Little Icaruses

As I unscrew the dead
60-watt bulb and shake
your bodies from the glass globe
into the trash, I feel
huge, like God
or science. As I screw in
the new sun, I blink,
descend, fold up
the stepladder. It's time
to paint on new lips
and drive out
into the risky neon mist.

Violenza Sessuale

There is a man with a purple beard—
a *viola* (in Italian) beard. A viola (in English)
under his chin. He is playing a song
full of violence, his head bobbing,
his purple whiskers tangled in the strings.
He whispers, *"violenza sessuale,"*
a sensual violence, an Italian euphemism for rape.
He is Bluebird, but purple. He is purple prose
with a Purple Heart even though his bow
saws away at the viola's strings,
saws away at his own wounds and hers,
until there isn't music anymore.

My Strip Club

In my strip club
the girls crawl on stage
wearing overalls
and turtlenecks
then slowly pull on
gloves, ski masks,
and hiking boots.
As the music slows,
they lick the pole
and for a tantalizing second
their tongues stick
because it's so cold.
They zip up parkas
and tie tight bows
under their hoods.
A big spender
can take one of my girls
into a back room
where he can clamp
on her snowshoes.

Victor

loneliness is holding a piece of cardboard
under your new kitchen cabinets
as the handyman drills holes for the hinges
that will hold the door in place
and you are catching the sawdust
so he won't make a mess
as he looks down your blouse and asks you to lunch
I know you like lunch and you say you can't
and he presses *why not* and *aw come on*
until he says *don't tell me you have a new man already*
and you say *Victor* a name you make up on the spot

your handyman says *take it from me I'm divorced twice
it's too early to date exclusively* and you say
I hear you but Victor is really something
this is the last trip your handyman needs to make
to finish the job he started four months ago
when your ex was trying to get alimony
from you and the handyman said *no man should take money
from a girl* and *that's really low* and you loved him
for being on your side and paid him cash
under the table and he was always on time
and swept up because he'd been a single dad

your therapist will tell you later you chose the name *Victor*
because it means champion winner conqueror
but for now you are holding on
as best as you can resisting the handyman
whom you actually like but everyone you trust
has said *don't do it* and *you deserve better*
because the handyman is a bankrupt chain-smoking alcoholic

who's looking for a place to live
most probably with you
a sober employed woman allergic to smoke
and you are thinking *what do my friends know*

when the handyman says *let's take a shower together*
and see what happens you almost drop the cardboard
and the mound of sawdust
that you wish didn't look so much like a mound
and you say *are you crazy* and the handyman sulks
well it was worth a try and you ask
why did you wait so long to ask me out
knowing he would have had a much better chance
when he first started the tile work
and you probably would have given anything
just to have someone hold you

when he says *I wanted it to be all proper*
so that we could see each other
me not working for you anymore
you give him the last beer in your fridge
that you've kept stocked just for him
and he folds the bubble wrap
the doors were swaddled in saying *keep this*
I know you like bubble wrap, which seems like
the most romantic thing anyone has ever said
to you and that this handyman knows you
better than any other man ever has

when he folds up the cardboard packaging
to take out to the trash you follow him

trying to think of something that would make him laugh
when he leaves he shakes your hand
and says *just for the record I hate Victor's guts*
and you almost say *me too*

You Don't Get to Tell Me What to Do Ever Again

—Lester Burnham

There was a time all my husband wanted was sex.
I was premenstrual, too tired,
in a bitch of a mood, then perimenopausal,
or maybe even bored.
He would lie beside me jerking off
while I pretended to be asleep.
Maybe he saw a neighborhood cheerleader
suspended on the ceiling like Kevin Spacey did,
which made me the uptight Annette Bening.
Whom did I want to have sex with then, if not him?
There were wild crushes I never let get out of hand
even though one time I spent the night
at someone else's apartment
but alone on a couch. My husband was oddly cool
about it. He said *I know you are having an affair,*
almost pleased, as though now he was off the hook
to make me happy.
                    The year before he left
we avoided being awake in bed
at the same time and, when we were,
we lay on our backs hoping the other would take over.
One night I turned on my side, facing the wall,
remembering the way we used to kiss, the eager way
all lovers kiss at first, then the way the kisses fizzle
and shorten to a peck.
                    I took a deep breath, tried
to formulate something loving or seductive to say,
but instead snapped, *Will you please stop that!*
and my husband's secret was out. He left the bed
for the bathroom and the recliner

and eventually for another woman in another state,
which leads me to today. Now that it's too late,
all I want is sex. I am the one jerking off
as the hands of my imagined and real lovers,
dead or gone, reach down from the ceiling
sprinkling me with rose petals, red *American Beauty* mouths
that whisper *there's no way to domesticate you, darling,*
and I pretend I can do whatever I want.

Self-Portrait in Hydrogen Peroxide

I never thought of myself as "the blonde" or even "a blonde,"
until a young man working his way up
to asking me for a date says, *My ex is jealous of the blonde*
I keep talking about. At first, I think he means someone else,
someone other than me. A third woman in the equation.
Then he says, *My friends want to know why I keep bringing up*
the blonde divorcée. I have only recently grasped the fact
that I am a divorcée, the gentle accent over the first *e*
like a hand coming down to pat me on the shoulder,
to tell me things will be OK. I don't have to be ostracized,
like the divorced moms I knew as a child. I'm a cougar now,
accepted and absorbed by the mainstream,
even though I haven't had plastic surgery, even though
my bank account isn't exactly purring. I get this, sort of,
but I still don't feel like a blonde. In fact,
I dyed my hair red for over ten years, until I moved to Florida
where it was too hard to keep up, my frizz turning orange in the sun.
So I went back to being blonde, but not "a blonde" or "the blonde."
I insisted on Jodie-Foster-ash-blonde, not Pamela-Anderson-platinum,
the first choice of the hairdresser who was sure
I could pull it off. I grew up with dumb blonde jokes
and one of my big fears was looking stupid. Another big fear,
looking smart. I had the highest IQ in 7th grade—
the teacher announced this fact to the class
after we took some standardized test. Great, I thought,
now I'll never get a date. So I tried to act dumb,
then smart again, then I thought that what I really wanted
was to blend in, but that can't be true—
because why would I have dyed my hair bright red?
It was an experiment for an article I was writing
for an alternative weekly in New York,

to see if people reacted to redheads differently,
which, I found, they did. Women were less likely to cut
in front of me in line, men less likely to whistle.
I held onto my power in a Clairol box as long as I could.
But now I have a lot of gray hair. To tell you the truth,
it's easier to be blonde because the gray blends in,
just the way I've always wanted to blend in
and not. The magazine folded, so my article was never printed.
Glamour ran a similar story shortly thereafter,
blondes on staff becoming redheads and brunettes, reporting pretty
much the same results I'd found. Now I'm middle-aged,
with a middle-age spread. Even though I'm "a blonde,"
it's false advertising. *There's a lot of silver in my hair,*
I tell my potential suitor. He says he doesn't care, reminding me
that I am a cougar, which makes him a cub. I catch us
in the mirror—my lines, my loose skin, a wrinkle
in my skirt, his big arms and pressed shirt. I'm nervous
and talking too much, about my doomed
article on redheads for which I was paid a kill fee,
a term I have to explain. He's relieved
I'm not a murderer. When I ask him if he knows
what a cub reporter is, he squints. *I'm 47,* I blurt.
He says, *Oh, never mind then, you crazy old lady.*
Why would I want to go out with you?
Then I begin to roar, the big laugh of a blonde cougar.

Proposal

I became a reverend
online so that I could marry
my niece and her fiancé
who didn't want
a traditional wedding

I became a reverend
shortly after my divorce
as the Universal Life Church
doesn't care about a cleric's
marital status and neither did
my niece

       when I told her
I was afraid to bring her
bad luck she would have
none of that and besides
who better to officiate
than someone who knew
the pitfalls of relationships

I could keep an eye
on the new couple
and they could come to me
and I'd know
the warning signs I'd missed
in my own home and my niece
believed in marriage
and me regardless
of my failures and her fiancé nodded

and I told all this
to my friend Bruce
who was getting divorced himself

I was at the beginning
of one marriage (as a reverend)
and at the end of another
(as a spouse) perfectly poised
to let him know
it was all going to be OK
when he said *I bet you can't wait*
to marry someone now that you can

I said *you must be kidding*
I'll never get married again
and he said *what I mean is*
I bet you can't wait
to marry another couple

Ten Days before We Meet, I Dream You

I remember him as always having
a tan, this guy I longed for
in high school, whose affections
I misunderstood, who
became my good friend
only to tell me how he was in love
with Sally. *How could he make her
like him?* He stood against a brick wall,
smoking, as I gave him advice—
good advice, as it never occurred to me
to undermine his efforts. (But now, in this dream,
he wants me, as though he was mistaken
all those years ago.

       He's still that teenager
though I've grown to middle age.
But now, in this dream, there are splashes
of freckles on his forehead,
blonde hair on his arms. Maybe he isn't
the boy I first thought he was. "What happened
to your tan?" I ask. He says, "You
married the wrong person."
He lays me on a bed and puts his hands
up my skirt. We make a fuzzy and abstract
kind of love, as though his body
and mine are vapor and haze.
Maybe I don't even have a body anymore.
But he does. I can see his chest and legs, freckles
across his brow as though someone has thrown
confetti at us.)

       I remember the story
from our high school reunion—

Sally in the emergency room,
beaten until she miscarried.
The boy I gave advice to, the boy
who'd convince Sally to marry him—
how could he have become that man?
Why didn't I tell him I liked him?
If I'd convinced him to like me,
would he have beaten me
instead of Sally?

      I instructed the boy to put a flower
in Sally's locker. When I saw him
a few years after they were married,
he asked me out for a drink.
I didn't go, not because I was that virtuous,
or loyal to Sally, but because by then
I'd lost interest in this boy/man
stocking shelves at the supermarket.
I felt superior since I was in college
and sad for him at the same time. I didn't know
what I was escaping.
      (Later in the dream
I figure out he can't be the boy
I thought he first was—no tan,
no meanness. I knew he was someone important
to the plot and I told him that.
He was wearing an iPod
and put one of the buds in my ear.
There were lyrics—something about a girl
having to isolate herself,
move far away. Maybe the song
was about me, what I'd done.

Maybe the song was about a girl
the boy in my dream once loved.
Only when he rolled off of me
did he age into a man.
I began to pull the sheets
from what looked at first like a stretcher,
then a twin bed. When he said
we'd see each other again soon, I kissed him
for good luck.) My alarm
sounded like a siren
on a rescue truck.

I Read

the heart beats 100,000 times a day, which leads me to think I could write a poem 100,000 words long, each word a beat, each beat how I feel about you. Each word would have two syllables, words mimicking tic-toc, ocean, thunk-thunk—trochee, iamb, a few spondees thrown in for when I'm really pounding. I do the math and realize my potential poem will be 300 pages, no punctuation or sentences, only word after word— and it will probably take you a whole day to read, a full 24 hours, and the poem will probably make sense only if you read it all in one sitting. So then when would you sleep? And why would you take the time to read such a poem-beast when you could just put your hand on the skin right over my heart? And why would I take time to write 100,000 words when everything I want to say is already said when you pledge your allegiance? Da-dum. Arise. Vroom-vroom. Beep-beep.

Long Distance Relationship

Dan said setting up a household
as man and woman
doesn't do either any good
I knew he was right
but still I was sad
missing you 1,172 miles away
once you joked
you'd fold up the earth
so that Delaware, Ohio
would be only one town
from Hollywood, Florida
and it occurs to me
that it could be worse
you could be in the state
of Delaware and I could be
in Hollywood, California
and then there'd be time zones
to contend with
and sometimes one of us would be
in the dark while the other
was in the light
when I told my GYN about you
he said we were G.U.
geographically undesirable
a term I'd never heard
he was married and I thought
how does he know the codes
of modern dating
was he a cheater
or did patients like me
tell him their woes

how they missed their G.U.'s
the way I miss not being
with you and your daughter Emmy
who told the story
of one of her students
who called the gynecologist
a vaginacologist
several times before she got
what he was saying
and that even as she corrected him
she had to admit
that the vaginacologist
as a word made sense
and I tell my GYN
all about it as he writes
me a prescription
for a bone density
and mammogram
at the clinic
where the technician gives me
a pink carnation
like she does every year
I usually forget it
on the back seat of the car
where it browns
but today I bring it inside
to put in water
so that when you
get off the plane tomorrow
I can give you a boutonnière

Sleep Seeds

I read about a mother who licked
her infant daughter's
eyes open, washed away
the sleep seeds
with her tongue.
This must have been
a woman without a facecloth
or warm water, a child
with terrible allergies.
This must have had
something to do
with poverty. Or maybe
I was reading about
the grooming habits of gorillas
or chimps.
                    I have asked you
to blow dust away
from my lower lid. I have
pressed the open parenthesis
of a lash from your cheek
onto my fingertip
and kept it. And if, one morning,
you wake but cannot
see me, I will also
be the woman who laps
your glued eyelids
until they part. I will ease
away each sleep seed,
each tear's unbeautiful sister.
Though I can't remember

if the mother and daughter
were from a magazine article
or novel or poem,
the gesture has stayed with me.
Back then, before I met you,
I thought *gross.*

                Now I think *love—*
our eyes forming crystals
and diamonds when we dream.

Having a Diet Coke with You

is even more fun than going to the spa in Mexico where I get three free massages—
hand, scalp, foot—in return for teaching a poetry class to which only two people
show up since it's scheduled against water aerobics so I barely have to work

I want us to sip fountain drinks sitting on stools at a diner counter
to be discovered like people used to be discovered
but instead of starring in movies we'll go on to star in poems

what I'm trying to say is I love you
partly because you taste better than the blueberry smoothies
I'd get every day at 3 p.m. after my writing workshop
partly because you are the smartest person I've ever met
and I want to ask what it is like to work on a farm or groom a horse
partly because I want to slide into your head and swim there
surely I can find a slit
right where your skin and hairline meet
so I can paddle around in your brain
partly because of the way you flex your arm

it is hard to believe I am writing a love poem
after years of telling my students
who wants to read about your giddy happiness
meaning I suppose that I didn't want to read about their giddy happiness
and I would announce with great authority
that love poems are the most difficult poems to write
because each love poem contains its opposite its loss
and that no matter how fierce the love of a couple
one of them will leave the other
if not through betrayal
then through death

last semester a young student sulked
thanks a lot for that information and I felt like an asshole
because even though I was mostly right
I shouldn't have pissed all over her goofy ode to her boyfriend that
though not a piece of literature
meant a lot to her and I actually apologized after class
and wished her well and said *don't listen to me*
what do I know about love

I told myself starting out that I was going to use Frank O'Hara's
"Having a Coke with You" to model this poem
he has four lines that begin with "partly because" too
but after the anaphora I could no longer follow his path
and I broke away from his form but not from his essence

O'Hara in his manifesto *Personism*
one time thinking about his sweetheart realized he
"could use the telephone instead of writing the poem"
and so I think you and I have been talking
our collaborative poems with each Skype encounter
the blue-clouded *S* icon resting at the bottom of my screen and yours
the way I want you to rest your head on my pillow
and why would I want to go to a museum in Florence or Bilbao
or anywhere else when I have your face to study

in O'Hara's poem he wants to take his lover to the Frick
since the lover has never been and Frank wants to see each painting again
through his new guy's eyes just as I want to take you to the boardwalk
where you have never strolled and to the empty lifeguard hut
against which you have never sat
we can climb up the ramp at night

and if we wake up early enough we can bike
to the turtle park where mothers lay their eggs and a woman from the city
comes to pick the hatchlings out of the sand to bring them to the ocean
because the baby turtles are confused by the lights
from all the development on the beach and often can't figure out
their way back to the sea
I want to pick you up if you lose your way
and carry you in the same kind of bucket she hauls with her fists
I want to take you to a safe place which is not to say
you are a baby but rather to say you are my baby, baby

that comma is the first and only comma in this poem
and I hope you will forgive this punctuation mark that doesn't quite fit
but I want you to pause on the second mention of the word *baby*
as though it is the sexiest word you've ever heard
earlier tonight my friend Barbra said *I can't wait to read your love poems
for Robert* and I said *I'm not sure I can write any
because I don't think I can do him justice*

what I'm trying to say is I love you
partly because you ripped up the carpet to prepare for my visit
when I told you I was allergic to your dog
partly because I want to be more like you
you are so much of your own nature
while I sometimes feel so far away from mine
partly because when you read me the first pages of your new novel
and I scanned ahead eager to get to the next sentence
you let me turn away from the monitor and toward you
so I could just listen to your voice
partly because you know so much about animals and I was always so afraid
of them not only because of my asthma and the dander

but also because animals didn't talk
and I couldn't tell what they were thinking
partly because you were in the real Mexico to research your book
while I was in the fake rich-people Mexico
where I didn't fit in where I was clearly the help
and I wish now I could have been with you
even though we hadn't yet met
partly because of the way you shared your iPod
one earbud in your ear the other in mine
partly because you said the word *aplomb* with such aplomb

my poem is already much longer than O'Hara's
now with an extra stanza of "partly because" lines
I'm not sure if you know this poem of his
or if anyone reads it anymore
I'm not sure Diet Coke was even invented when he wrote it
if he wanted a diet drink he probably had to endure Tab
there was no Diet Coke allowed at the spa
too many chemicals
but I know if you'd been with me in Mexico
we would have snuck some in because you make me want to break rules
I suggested a bridesmaid read O'Hara's poem at my niece's wedding
but she and her fiancé didn't think it was quite romantic enough
and went for Pablo Neruda and e.e. cummings
you can't go wrong with those two I know
but this O'Hara love poem has been lingering in me
waiting for you to come along so I could share it

I remember hiking to the organic farm at the spa
a few miles up the mountain to hear the lecture about the seed bank
that stored the ancient lettuce and squashes

and you seem to me now like one of those seeds
that almost went extinct but didn't
I'm resisting the temptation to transplant
everything you've told me here
because some things I want to be just for us
and there it is I suppose the problem
with all narrative postconfessional transgressive poetry
whatever this kind of poetry is referred to as in this moment
how to keep loyal to the art without being disloyal
to the love and what to tell and what to hold back

what I am trying to say is I love you wholly/holy
what I am trying to say is holy moley
what I am trying to say is that while I know
love poems are the hardest poems
and I know one of us will go
before the other still I am stepping with you into the sea
where other lovers have performed for each other
doing somersaults or handstands
their palms in the pebbles and muck
until the waves flipped them over

I remember crying at the spa during my scalp massage
the masseuse's hands were so tender I sniveled into the sheet
she explained that this sort of outburst happened a lot
to women who weren't used to being touched with kindness
or maybe that's not what she said
she was speaking rapid Spanish and I couldn't keep up
that may have just been what I wanted to hear
when you washed my hair one of our first nights together
I thought of her and wanted to tell you this story

but there were so many stories I couldn't squeeze it in
when you touched my fingers my feet
I wanted to call this woman in Mexico
to say *thank you* or *gracias* but I don't even know her name

I'm not sure if you know the artist Marino Marini
but O'Hara says "he didn't pick the rider as carefully / as the horse"
Marini's *Great Horse* is in the Rockefeller Collection in New York
do you want to go see it together in December
I know I said I don't need art anymore only your face
and though that is still true I know you love horses
I don't really know much
about them except that they eat whole apples

I also know I said I wanted us to be discovered
spinning on our stools in a Woolworth's that no longer exists
drinking our Diet Cokes out of frosted glass tumblers loaded with ice
but I think what I really meant is that I want us
to discover each other

after we finish our Diet Cokes
I want to pack a basket lined with red gingham cloth
to take you on a picnic
and share an apple with you
slicing off chunks with a knife
or just passing it back and forth taking bites
while you tell me everything you know

please tell me you'll go

Ode to Your Eyebrows

They are, my love, a cross
between Einstein's and wheat fields.
Twin mustaches. Strands of sugar
right before the cotton candy is spun.
Astroturf welcome mats. The cellophane grass
of Easter baskets. Caterpillar chia pets.
Brambles and squiggles.
Seaweed strewn on shore.
Spiky cloud tufts
that lift up
when I show you
my slip
or my smarts.

ACKNOWLEDGMENTS

Grateful acknowledgement is made to the editors and staff members of the magazines, chapbooks, and anthologies in which these poems, sometimes in different versions, first appeared:

American Poetry Review ("A Different Story"); *Barrow Street* ("How It Will End"); *Bloomsbury Review* ("Courtship"); *Chatauqua Review* ("Worst Case Scenerio"); *Collagist* ("Sleep Seeds"); *Conclave: A Journal of Character* ("My Shortcut"); *Court Green* ("Long Distance Relationship" and "You Don't Get to Tell Me What to do Ever Again"); *DMQ Review* ("My Strip Club"); *5 a.m.* ("Recession Commandments"—with the title "Recession Decalogue"—and "Loaded"); *Fogged Clarity* ("Ten Days before We Meet, I Dream You"); *Freelunch* ("Duper's Delight"); *Harvard Review* ("If You Really Want to" and "Tina and the Bruised Hearts"); *Hotel Amerika* ("My New Chum"); *Indiana Review* ("I Read"); *Luna* ("You're Looking at the Love Interest"); *Marsh Hawk Review* ("*Voilenza Sussuale*"); *Mid-American Review* ("Having a Diet Coke with You"); *Normal School* ("Or Wherever Your Final Destinaion May Be"); *New Ohio Review* ("Takeout, 2008" and "Old Love Poems"); *New Yizner* ("The Widow"); *One Trick Pony* ("Mack"); *Oranges and Sardines* ("Self-Portrait in Hydrogen Peroxide"); *Paterson Literary Review* ("Cleopatra Invented the First Vibrator"); *Ploughshares* ("Ode to Your Eyebrows"); *Prairie Schooner* ("And So"); *Quarterly West* ("Victor"); *Salt Hill Review* ("Expired"); *Same* ("Little Icaruses"); *Saw Palm Florida Literature and Art* ("Madonna and Me" and "*Heartburn*"—with the title "Food and Men"); *Shenandoah* ("*An Unmarried Woman*" and "Lower East Side Boyfriend"); *Tigertail, a South Florida Annual* ("Ritual"); *Verse Wisconsin* ("Kindergarten Boyfriend," "Fourth Grade Boyfriend," and "Proposal").

"If You Really Want To" was reprinted in the *1 Cent Journal*. "My Shortcut" was reprinted in *OWL*.

"Duper's Delight," "If You Really Want to," "Madonna and Me," "Takeout, 2008," *Heartburn*," "Self-Portrait in Hydrogen Peroxide," "Victor," and "How It Will End" also appear in the e-chapbook *How It Will End* (Floating Wolf Quarterly Chapbooks, 2010).

"Madonna and Me," "I Read," "My Shortcut," "Expired," "Victor," and "How It Will End" also appear in *Enjoy Hot or Iced: Poems in Conversation and a Conversation* (Slapering Hol Press, 2011).

"How It Will End" was reprinted in *The Best American Poetry 2009*, edited by David Lehman and David Wagoner (Simon and Schuster, 2009), *Poetry: An Introduction*, edited by Michael Meyer (Bedford / St. Martin's, 2009), and in *The Best of the Best American Poetry: 1988–2012*, edited by David Lehman and Robert Pinsky (Scribner, 2013).

"My Strip Club" was reprinted in the *The Best American Poetry 2011*, edited by David Lehman and Kevin Young (Scribner, 2011).

"Or Wherever Your Final Destination May Be" was reprinted in *The Unbearables Big Book of Sex*, edited by Ron Kolm, et al. (Autonomedia, 2011).

"Mack" is dedicated to Louis McKee. "The Widow" is dedicated to Noelle Kocot.

With many thanks to Stephanie Strickland, who guided me in rethinking individual poems and titles, and to Florida International University's Department of English and the College of Arts and Sciences for their support and funding for travel. And with tremendous gratitude to Ed Ochester and all the kind and creative people at the University of Pittsburgh Press.